W9-AXB-972

Volume 5
Chemistry

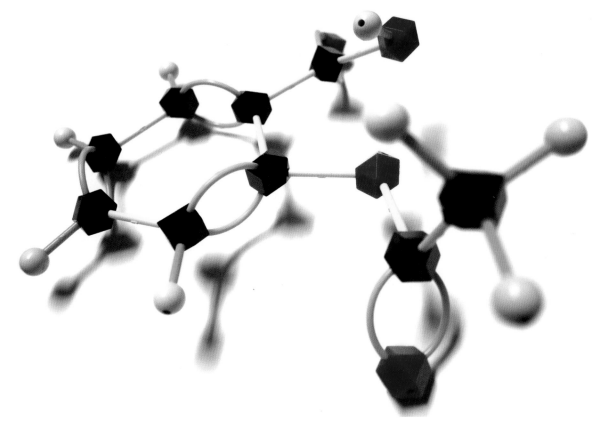

By Nancy Harris

Editorial Consultant
Luana Mitten
Project Editor
Kurt Sturm

Rourke
Publishing LLC
Vero Beach, Florida 32964

www.rourkepublishing.com

Photo credits: Page 4 © Lisa F. Young; Page 4b © Denis Pepin; Page 4c © Roman Sigaev; Page 4d © ASP; Page 5 © Stavchansky Yakov; Page 5b © EcoPrint; Page 6 © Emin Kuliyev; Page 6b © Scott Bauer; Page 6c © Kiselev Andrey Valerevich; Page 7 © Oliver Hoffmann; Page 7b © Kiselev Andrey Valerevich; Page 7c © Emin Kuliyev; Page 7d © Anyka; Page 8 © Dragan Trifunovic; Page 9 © Nikola Hristovski; Page 9b © NASA; Page 10 © Ron Hilton; Page 10b © mmm; Page 11 © U.S. Department of Defense; Page 12 © Leo; Page 13 © U.S. Department of Energy; Page 13b © Courtesy of Brookhaven National Laboratory; Page 14 © Steffen Foerster Photography; Page 14b © Jon Zander; Page 14c © Carsten Reisinger; Page 15 © Ilya D. Gridnev; Page 16 © Michael Dayah, www.ptable.com; Page 17 © Michael Dayah, www.ptable.com; Page 18 © Clarence S Lewis; Page 18b © Jorge Pedro Barradas de Casais; Page 18c © Konovalikov Andrey; Page 19 © Lorelyn Medina; Page 20 © Scott Bauer - USDA; Page 22 © Zsoit Nyulaszi; Page 22b © Tracy Lee Didas; Page 24 © vm; Page 24b © Giovanni Bernintende; Page 25 © Michael J. Thompson; Page 25b © Ivaschenko Roman; Page 26 © Joana Drutu; Page 28 © Sz Akos; Page 29 © PhotoCreate; Page 29b © Shironina Lidiya Alexandrovna; Page 29c © Zaichenko Olga; Page 29d © Can Balcioglu; Page 30 © Stephane Tougard; Page 30b © Rebecca Abell; Page 30c © Dr. Morley Read; Page 31 © DigitalLife; Page 31b © David Lee; Page 32 © Artsilense; Page 32b © PhotoDisc ; Page 32c © NASA; Page 33 © Gordana Sermek; Page 33b © Olivier Le Queinec; Page 33c © Ingrid Balabanova; Page 34 © Andreas Gradin; Page 34b © Vera Bogaerts; Page 34c © PhotoDisc; Page 35 © Leonid Smirnov; Page 35b © Nicholas James Homrich; Page 35c © Losevsky Pavel; Page 36 © Jason Stitt; Page 36b © Andraz Cerar; Page 37 © hd connelly; Page 37b © Vuk Vukmirovic; Page 37c © Robert Taylor; Page 38 © Dellison; Page 38b © Michael Rolands; Page 38c © Vladimir Sazonov; Page 39 © Peter Witkop; Page 39b © Joel Shawn; Page 39c © Michael Ledray; Page 40 © Sonya Etchison; Page 40b © Saniphoto; Page 41 © Charles Allen; Page 41b © Sir Thomas Lawrence; Page 42 © Kamarulzaman Russali; Page 42b © Michael Ledray; Page 43 © Elena Blokhina; Page 43b © Graca Victoria; Page 44 © Vicente Barcelo Varona; Page 44b © hd connelly; Page 45 © Robyn Mackenzie; Page 45b © Richard Thornton; Page 45c © Sean Lean Tung Pek; Page 46 © Nicolaas Weber; Page 46b © Nicole Weiss; Page 47 © Sklep Spozywczy; Page 47b © Sai Yeung Chan; Page 48 © Shannon Workman; Page 48b © Alex; Page 49 © Scott Bauer - USDA; Page 50 © Fedorenko Oleg Nikolaevich; Page 51 © David M. Albrecht; Page 51b © NASA; Page 52 © Keely Deuschle; Page 52b © Kris Butler; Page 53 © Oshchepkov Dmitry; Page 53b © Peter Gudella; Page 53c © Michael Onisforou; Page 54 © NASA; Page 54b © Micah May; Page 55b © Frances L Fruit; Page 56 © Micah May; Page 56b © Frank Anusewicz ; Page 57 © Kamarulzaman Russali; Page 58 © Polina Lobanova; Page 58b © Dori O'Connell;Page 58c © Dragan Trifunovic; Page 59 © Anyka; Page 60 © Trout55; Page 60b © ARTSILENSEcom; Page 60c © DJ Images; Page 60d © PhotoDisc; Page 60e © Lorelyn Medina; Page 61 © Laser222; Page 61b © ASP; Page 61c © Olga Zaporozhskaya; Page 61d © Kamarulzaman Russali; Page 61e © Janprchal; Page 62e © Courtesy: Pugwash Conferences on Science and World Affairs

Editor: Luana Mitten

Cover design by Nicola Stratford. Blue Door Publishing

Library of Congress Cataloging-in-Publication Data

Rourke's world of science encyclopedia / Marcia Freeman ... [et al.].
     v. cm.
   Includes bibliographical references and index.
   Contents: [1] Human life --
   ISBN 978-1-60044-646-7
   1. Science--Encyclopedias, Juvenile. 2. Technology--Encyclopedias, Juvenile. I. Freeman, Marcia S. (Marcia Sheehan), 1937-
Q121.R78 2008
503--dc22

                          2007042493

Volume 5 of 10
ISBN 978-1-60044-651-1

Printed and bound in China through Sino Publishing House Ltd.

CG/CG

Rourke Publishing

www.rourkepublishing.com – rourke@rourkepublishing.com
Post Office Box 3328, Vero Beach, FL 32964

Table of Contents

What is Chemistry? 4
  The Scientific Method 5
  Measurement 8

Atoms and Elements 11
  The Parts of an Atom 12
  Elements 14
  The Periodic Table 16
  Elements Important to Life .19
  Isotopes and Radioactive Elements 20

Molecules 24
  Bonds 25
  Chemical Formulas 28

Matter 29
  Phases of Matter 29
  Properties of Matter 31
  Changes in Matter 38

Compounds, Acids and Bases, Mixtures, and Solutions 40
  Compounds 41
  Acids and Bases 42
  Mixtures 45
  Solutions 46

Reactions 48
  Chemical Reactions 48
  Making and Breaking Bonds 49
  Catalysts 49
  Oxidation and Reduction 52
  Releasing Energy 55
  Explosions 56

People Who Study Chemistry 59
  Types of Chemists 59
  Women in Chemistry 62

What Is Chemistry?

Chemistry is the study of substances and the changes that happen to them. Substances are things like food, clothes, and medicine.

Chemistry is very important. Plastic bags and shoes with rubber soles would not exist without chemistry. Fuels for cars, airplanes, and rockets would not exist without chemistry. Chemical reactions, or changes, inside the human body are important. They make it possible for people to think, eat, and breathe. Chemistry is everywhere.

Chemicals in fertilizer helped these fruits and vegetables grow.

Without chemistry, we would not have these clothes to keep us warm.

Enzymes in the girls' stomachs will help them digest their food.

We know how our medicine works because of chemistry.

Find out more

What do elephant tusks and billiard balls have in common?

Before the invention of plastic, elephant tusks were the main material used to make billiard balls. John Wesley Hyatt invented celluloid, a special kind of plastic, in 1868. Celluloid proved to be the perfect ingredient for creating billiard balls as well as movie film.

The Scientific Method

Scientists learn about chemistry in three ways. They observe, or watch, substances. They study substances and they do experiments. They try to make substances change and then record what happens. Scientists carefully plan how they learn about chemistry. They often use a system called the scientific method to answer questions they might have.

The scientific method is very important. It allows scientists to learn about how things work. There are four parts to the scientific method:

1. Scientists begin the scientific method by asking a question.

2. They research information about their question, or problem. When gathering information, scientists use observation to watch what they are studying very carefully. They might write down, or record their observations when collecting the information. Scientists call this information data. They also collect data by reading other scientists' books and journal articles. The Internet is another useful tool for gathering information.

A scientist carefully records data during an experiment.

3. The third step of the scientific method is making a thoughtful guess, or hypothesis. A hypothesis is an idea or opinion based on some data or observations, but not proven.

Scientists formed the hypothesis that this fertilizer is what makes the plants grow big and healthy. They will test their hypothesis to see if it is true.

4. The fourth step of the scientific method is gathering materials and then testing the hypothesis. Scientists, test or try out, their hypotheses in experiments.

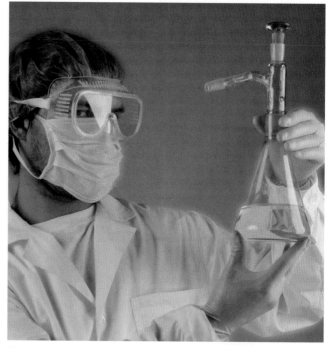

Scientists conduct the same experiment many times to be sure of the results.

Scientists often do their experiments in a laboratory. A laboratory is a place where scientists conduct experiments and collect data. Controlling conditions in a laboratory is easier than controlling conditions in the real world. For example, temperature levels are able to remain constant in a controlled setting. That would be impossible to do outside of a laboratory.

HOW DO SCIENTISTS LEARN ABOUT CHEMISTRY?

They observe or watch substances.

They do experiments.

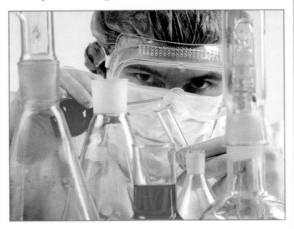

They try to make substances change and then record what happens.

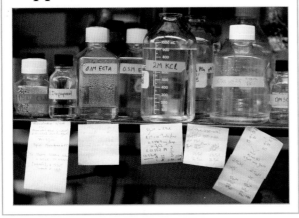

An experiment might show that the hypothesis is not correct. For this reason, scientists always perform tests for one experiment several times. They call these tests trials. In each trial, scientists change only one thing, also known as the variable. New data might cause a scientist to change the hypothesis. Sometimes, a scientist throws away the hypothesis and starts all over. Hypotheses proven true predict how things will work and can be very helpful.

Chemists made sure this medicine was safe for children.

control (kuhn-TROHL): to make something or someone do what you want

experiment (ek-SPER-uh-ment): a scientific test to try out a theory or to see the effect of something

fuel (FYOO-uhl): something that is used as a source of heat or energy, such as coal, wood, gasoline, or natural gas

observation (ob-zur-VAY-shuhn): the careful watching of someone or something

Measurement

People can describe the world in many ways. They can say how big something is, how much it weighs, or how hot it feels. They can use measurements to describe these things.

Scientists use the metric system to measure distance and length. They measure distance and length using a metric ruler, tape measure, or other special tools. A meter is a specific unit of measurement. A meter can be broken down into smaller parts called centimeters and millimeters. There are 100 centimeters (cm) in 1 meter (m). There are 1,000 millimeters (mm) in 1 meter. There are 1,000 meters in a kilometer (km).

Your dad measures your height in the standard unit of inches. Scientists measure height in the metric unit of centimeters.

Unit of Measurement	Abbreviation	Things You Might Measure With This Unit
millimeter	mm	ant, small button, or end of an eraser
centimeter	cm	hamster, length of your foot, or the length of a gecko lizard
meter	m	distance between your classroom and the lunchroom, or the length of a Komodo dragon or a whale
kilometer	km	distance of a marathon or the distance between two cities

Unit of Measurement	Abbreviation	Things You Might Measure With This Unit
kilogram	kg	yourself or a tiger
gram	g	a bag of apples or a box of cookies
milligram	mg	a paper clip or a baby tooth

Scientists use grams or milligrams to measure the weight of something. Scales are instruments used to measure weight. Scientists use scales that weigh in kilograms, grams or milligrams.

Find out more

What's the Difference Between Mass and Weight?

Weight is the measure of how strongly gravity pulls on matter. Mass is the measure of how much matter an object has. If you were to go to the Moon, your weight would change because the pull of gravity on Earth is stronger than on the Moon. Your mass would not change because you would still have the same amount of matter.

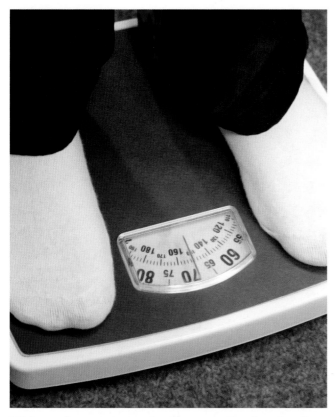

This scale measures in the standard unit of pounds or the metric unit of kilograms.

Scientists measure temperature using the Celsius temperature scale. The freezing and boiling points of water is the basis for Celsius (°C). Water freezes at 0°C and boils at 100°C. An average room temperature is about 20°C.

Another way of measuring temperature is to use the Kelvin scale. The lowest possible temperature determines the Kelvin (K) scale. This is 0 K or -273°C. Absolute temperatures are temperatures measured in the Kelvin scale.

Thermometers display temperature using the standard Fahrenheit scale and the metric Celsius scale.

distance (DISS-tuhnss): the amount of space between two places

length (lengkth): the distance from one end of something to the other

measure (MEZH-ur): to find out the size, capacity, weight, etc. of something

metric system (MET-rik SISS-tim): a system of measurement based on counting by 10's

temperature (TEM-put-uh-chur): the degree of heat or cold in something

Atoms and Elements

Atoms are the building blocks of all matter. Atoms are very small. Many atoms put together make up everything in the world. Atoms are so small that you cannot see an individual atom without a special microscope. All atoms are made of the same basic parts. Putting these parts together in different ways, by scientists or in nature, causes the traits of the atom to change.

Scientists use electron microscopes to give them an idea of what atoms look like.

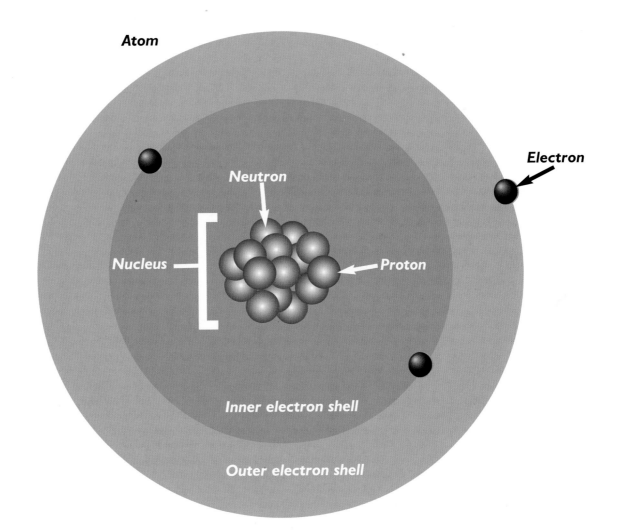

The Parts of an Atom

The parts inside the atom are much smaller than the atom itself. There are two sections in an atom. There is a center section and an outer section.

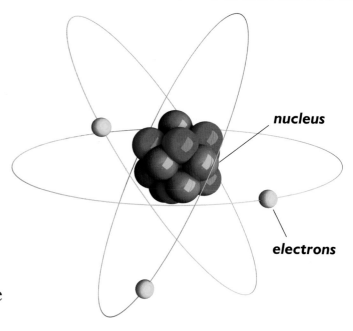

Center Section

The center section contains the nucleus. The nucleus is made of two types of particles. We call these particles protons and neutrons. Protons have a positive electrical charge. Neutrons do not have an electrical charge. Scientists say they are neutral. The nucleus of most common atoms is made of the same number of protons and neutrons.

Outer Section

The outer part of the atom is made of electrons. Electrons are very tiny particles. They move around the nucleus of an atom in special layers called shells. Each

shell can have several electrons in it. Many atoms have several electron shells. All electrons have a negative electrical charge. Normal atoms have the same number of electrons and protons. The negative electron and the positive proton attract. This is what holds the atom together.

Subatomic Particles

Subatomic particles exist inside an atom. Protons, neutrons, and electrons are examples of subatomic particles. Many other subatomic particles exist inside an atom. For example, protons and neutrons are made of tiny particles called quarks. Gluons, even smaller particles, hold quarks together. There are more than 200 other types of subatomic particles.

neutral (NU-trel): neither positive or negative

particle (PAR-tuh-kuhl): an extremely small piece or amount of something

trait (trate): a quality or characteristic that makes one person or thing different from another

Niels Bohr

Getting to know... Niels Bohr was born in Denmark in 1885. His father was a professor who invited many important scientists to their home. Bohr studied physics at the University of Copenhagen. Then he went to England to work with the famous physicists J.J. Thomson and Ernest Rutherford.

Bohr returned to Denmark and became a professor. He wrote papers in which he described the structure of an atom. Bohr showed that electrons have stable orbits around the nucleus, which allows them to keep spinning. Electrons give off energy only when they jump to a different orbit. In 1922, Bohr won the Nobel Prize for his studies of atoms.

Find out more

Scientists Can Smash Atoms

Particle accelerators are giant machines used by scientists to discover subatomic particles. These machines move atoms and subatomic particles very fast. Then they smash them together! Special photographs and computer images from the accelerator show the impact. The picture below shows the trails left by particles.

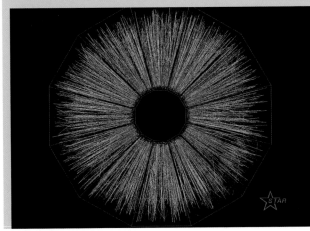

Elements

An element is a substance made of the same type of atoms. Scientists know of over 100 different elements. Most elements occur naturally. Some are very common. Others are harder to find. Scientists have created a few elements in laboratories.

Gold and copper are naturally occurring elements.

Solid Metals

Most of the elements are solid metals and usually shiny. They can also conduct, or pass on, heat and electricity. Metals are malleable and easily formed into many shapes.

Flattened sheets of metal used as prongs in an electrical cord conduct electricity. Pulling metals very thin without breaking them means they are ductile. Wires are an example of ductile metals.

The prongs on this electrical cord plugs into a wall. It will conduct the electricity to a lamp when switched on.

Nonmetals and Semimetals

The rest of the elements are nonmetals or semimetals. Nonmetals are different from metals in many ways. Most nonmetals are gases, like oxygen. Solid nonmetals are hard and brittle, like carbon. They break apart easily. Carbon is used to make some pencil tips. Bromine is the only liquid nonmetal. Semimetals have traits of both metals and nonmetals.

Helium is lighter than oxygen, allowing these balloons to float.

Atomic Number

Elements differ from one another depending on the number of protons each possesses. The number of protons in an element determines the atomic number of the element.

Protons and neutrons have about the same mass. Mass is the amount of physical material in an object. The atomic number determines the organization of all elements in the periodic table of elements. The first element, hydrogen is number one. The last known element, lawrencium, is number 103.

Protons and neutrons make up nearly all of the mass of an atom. The atomic mass of the element is the approximate total number of protons and neutrons in that element. The unit of measurement for atomic mass is the atomic mass unit (AMU).

Find out more How many neutrons are there in Krypton? The atomic number of Krypton is 36. This means there are 36 protons and 36 electrons in its nucleus. To determine the number of neutrons, you must first round the atomic weight. Krypton is about 84 AMU. Subtract the number of protons and that will leave us with the number of neutrons, 48.

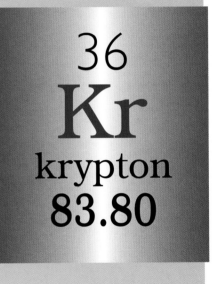

36
Kr
krypton
83.80

Use the table below to help find the number of protons, electrons, and neutrons of any element.

Number of Protons	Atomic Number
Number of Electrons	Atomic Number (or Number of Protons)
Number of Neutrons	Mass Number (rounded)- Atomic Number

The Periodic Table

Symbols

The periodic table lists all known elements. Each element has a special symbol that describes it. Some symbols are the first letter of the element. The first element has the letter H for hydrogen. O is for oxygen. C is for carbon. Most of the elements have a symbol with two letters. Helium has the letters He. Ca is the symbol for Calcium. Bromine is Br. Every element must have a different symbol, so sometimes the symbol is very different from the actual name of the element. Many of these symbols come from Latin words. Gold is Au. Tin is Sn. Silver is Ag.

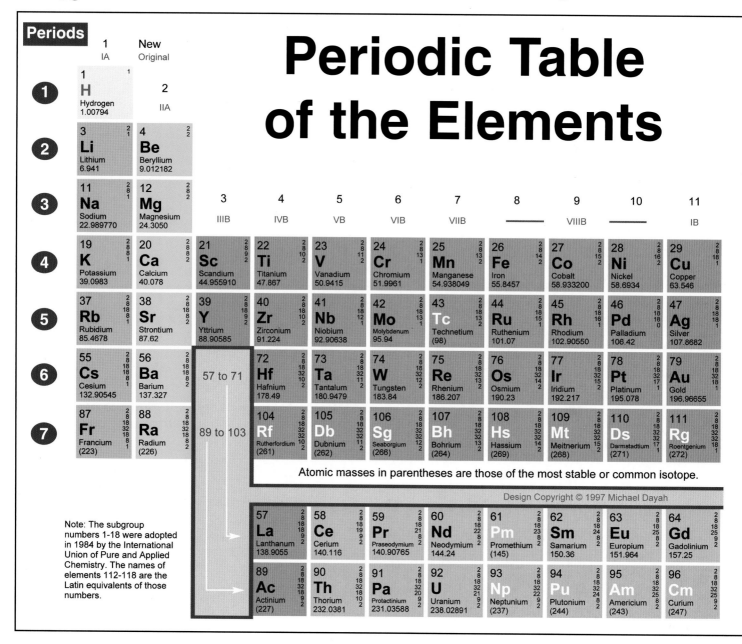

Periodic Table of the Elements

Atomic masses in parentheses are those of the most stable or common isotope.

Design Copyright © 1997 Michael Dayah

Note: The subgroup numbers 1-18 were adopted in 1984 by the International Union of Pure and Applied Chemistry. The names of elements 112-118 are the Latin equivalents of those numbers.

Listing Elements

The periodic table lists over 100 elements. The atomic number determines the arrangement of each element. Rows and columns help to organize the elements according to specific properties. A row going across is called a period. The atomic number in each period increases by one with each element as you move left to right across the table. The chemical properties of the elements change slowly as well. Each element contains one more electron and one more proton than the next. Columns, also known as groups, consist of elements that share similar chemical and physical properties.

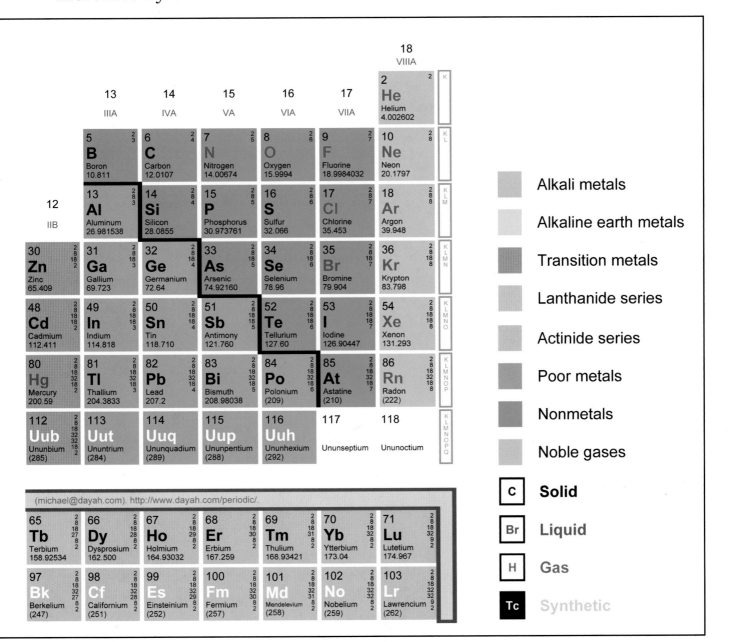

Alkali metals

Alkaline earth metals

Transition metals

Lanthanide series

Actinide series

Poor metals

Nonmetals

Noble gases

Solid

Liquid

Gas

Synthetic

(michael@dayah.com). http://www.dayah.com/periodic/.

Periods

Periods are the rows going across the periodic table of elements. As you move across the rows from left to right, the atomic number increases by one. This means that each element contains one more electron and one more proton than the previous element. The chemical and physical properties gradually change across the row. A new period begins with a drastic difference in properties.

As an example, the first period in the periodic table is very short. It contains only two elements, hydrogen (H) and helium (He). The second period contains eight elements. It begins with lithium (the symbol Li) and ends with neon (Ne). The fifth period also has 18 elements. It starts with rubidium (Rb) and ends with xenon (Xe). See chart on pages 16 and 17. Scientists are still discovering new elements.

Groups

Elements in the same group have similar properties. Every element in a group has the same number of electrons in its outer electron shell. With the exception of hydrogen, the elements in the first group, called alkali metals, each have only one electron in the outer shell. They are soft metals that react easily with water.

Noble gases are the last group. Helium, neon, argon, krypton, xenon, and radon are all noble gases. Except for helium, they all have eight electrons in their outer shells. They are usually inert elements. This means they do not combine chemically with other elements. In the 1960s, scientists were able to force noble gases to combine with other elements. The gases would otherwise not form a bond.

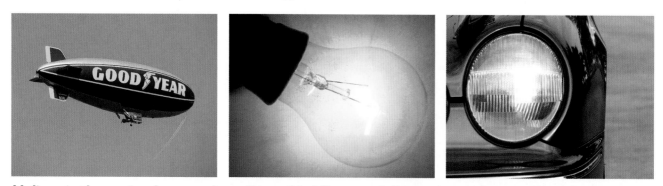

Helium is the main element that allows this blimp to defy gravity and stay afloat. Light bulbs stay lit because of argon. Headlights in this new car contain xenon.

Dmitry Mendeleyev

Getting to know... Dmitry Mendeleyev was born in 1834 in the country of Russia. His father became blind. His mother worked in a glass factory to support their fourteen children. In 1849, Mendeleyev left home to become a teacher.

Mendeleyev noticed that some elements have similar properties. He wondered if there was a way to classify elements, or place them into different groups. Using cards, Mendeleyev wrote down the properties of each element. He also wrote down the atomic weight of each element known at the time. He arranged the cards until he saw a pattern. Organizing the elements by their atomic weight allowed Mendeleyev to discover that the properties repeated themselves. Mendeleyev created the periodic table. Later, new elements filled empty spaces left in the table.

Elements Important to Life

On Earth, there are 92 naturally occurring elements. A few are the building blocks of all life on our planet. Hydrogen and oxygen form water. The atoms of five elements form the majority of the air we breathe. They are nitrogen, oxygen, carbon, hydrogen, and argon.

Elements mixed together form the surface of the Earth. These elements are mainly oxygen (O), silicone (Si), iron (Fe), aluminum (Al), and magnesium (Mg). Many scientists believe that the center, or core, of the Earth is made mainly of two elements. They are iron (Fe) and nickel (Ni).

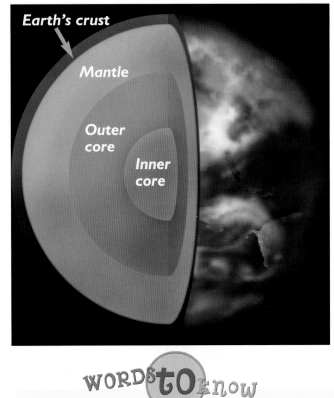

Earth's crust
Mantle
Outer core
Inner core

WORDS to know

Latin (LAT-uhn): the language of the ancient Romans

symbol (SIM-buhl): a design or object that represents something else

The same elements make up all organic or once living matter on Earth. The elements carbon, hydrogen, nitrogen, and oxygen, make up life on Earth. Plants and animals are exceptions. This is because the organization of the elements is different.

Life first developed when these and other elements came together millions of years ago. These elements exist throughout the universe. We do not know if life exists anywhere else.

Isotopes and Radioactive Elements

Isotopes

Sometimes, the nucleus of an atom can have extra neutrons. The normal atom and the one with extra neutrons have the same atomic numbers. This is because they have the same number of protons. They have different masses because of the extra neutrons. Scientists call these atoms isotopes.

All elements have isotopes. Many isotopes occur naturally. Some occur by themselves, like sodium. Other elements in nature are actually mixtures of several isotopes. Oxygen that occurs

naturally contains three isotopes of oxygen. It is a mixture containing mostly oxygen with an atomic mass of 16. It also has tiny amounts of oxygen with atomic masses of 17 and 18. Scientists can measure the mass of an atom by using a device called a mass spectrometer.

Mass spectrometry determines the effects of drugs in the body, identifies illegal steroids in an athlete, and determines the age and origin of once-living material in archeology.

ISOTOPES AND THEIR USES

Where They Are Used	Reasons for Their Use
Health and Medicine	For diagnosis of heart disease, cancer, and for therapy. Every year more than 30 million medical treatments and over 100 million laboratory tests are completed using isotopes.
Environment	For the measurement of air and water pollution and to understand the effects of radioactive waste on the public and environment.
Industrial Safety	Used to detect flaws in steel sections used for bridge and jet airliner construction.
Consumer Protection and Safety	Used to study the quality of food and its effect on humans.

Radioactive Isotopes

Carbon 12 is the most common isotope of carbon. It is stable because it has six neutrons and six protons. It has an atomic mass of 12. Carbon 14 is another isotope of carbon. It has two extra neutrons and an atomic mass of 14. Carbon 14 is an unstable or radioactive isotope of carbon. Some of its neutrons will break down into electrons and protons. Scientists call this radioactive decay. Measurement of radioactive decay is the amount of time that it takes carbon 14 to break down. Half-life is when half the nucleus in a sample of a radioactive isotope breaks down.

A radioactive isotope that is decaying gives off subatomic particles and rays. Scientists call this radiation.

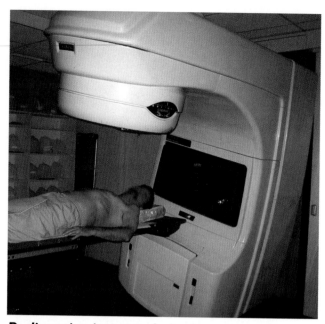

Radioactive isotopes help determine the health of patients and allow doctors to treat them more effectively.

Long-term exposure to radiation can cause cancer and blood diseases.

There are several tools used to detect radioactivity. The most well known tool is the Geiger counter. It will emit loud clicks or move a needle on a screen when encountering radioactive material.

For the past century, radioactive isotopes have become a part of our daily lives. We find them in smoke detectors, in the irradiation process that makes food safer, in carbon 14 dating which tells archeologists when an organism died, and often in the field of medicine. Doctors use radioactive isotopes, or tracers to identify diseases and treat them.

Doctors use radioactive isotopes, or tracers to identify diseases and treat them.

Radioactive elements and isotopes can also be harmful. A person exposed to too much radioactivity can develop radiation sickness. Their hair can fall out and they can become very ill.

This man uses a Geiger counter to determine the presence of radioactive materials.

The Disaster at Chernobyl

On April 26, 1986, one of four nuclear reactors exploded at the Chernobyl power station in Ukraine, a country that used to be a part of the old Soviet Union. The explosion burned for nine days, proving to be the worst nuclear accident in history. The disaster released at least 100 times more radiation than the atom bombs dropped in Nagasaki and Hiroshima. Much of the fallout fell close to Chernobyl, Belarus, Ukraine, and Russia. Many people left the area, but about 5.5 million people continue to live there today.

Every country in the Northern Hemisphere contains soil that has tested positive for traces of radioactive deposits from the Chernobyl disaster. No one knows the final number of people who will die as a result of this accident. Scientists and doctors in the area have seen a drastic increase in thyroid cancer, mainly in people who were children or teens at the time of the accident. Fortunately, survival rates are high in the case of this type of cancer. Today, work continues to keep the Chernobyl plant from crumbling. Wild horses, boar, wolves, and birds have returned to the area and are thriving.

Marie Curie

Marie Curie was born Marya Sklodowska in Poland in 1867. She attended the famous university in Paris called the Sorbonne. She married Pierre Curie in 1895. They studied chemistry together.

Marie and Pierre Curie heard that the element uranium gives off radiation. Uranium comes from an ore, which is a type of rock called pitchblende. They found two other radioactive elements in the pitchblende. They were polonium and radium.

In 1903, the Curies shared the Nobel Prize in Physics for their work with radioactivity. Pierre died in an accident in 1906, and Marie continued her research. She won the 1911 Nobel Prize in Chemistry for discovering polonium and radium. Marie Curie died of a type of cancer called leukemia. Exposure to radioactivity caused her cancer.

Molecules

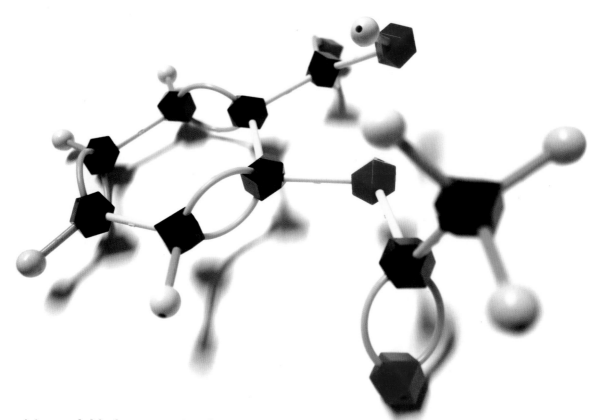

An aspirin model helps us to visualize what the actual molecule might look like.

Naturally occurring elements are usually a combination of several elements. Some combine with elements just like themselves. Others combine with different elements. Scientists call these combinations of elements molecules. They are made of at least two atoms and are stable. This means they have the same number of protons and neutrons.

A molecule is the smallest form of a substance that can exist on its own. A molecule still has the features of that substance.

Molecules can exist without breaking apart or linking to other atoms.

There are more molecules in your body than there are stars in the entire universe.

For some elements, there is no difference between a single atom and a molecule of the elements. For example, an atom of hydrogen is the same as a molecule of hydrogen. All the noble gases can exist as a molecule with a single atom. Noble gases include helium, neon, argon, krypton, xenon, and radon.

Bonds

A bond is like a link that holds two or more atoms together. There are many different kinds of bonds. Sometimes, atoms share electron pairs with other atoms. Scientists call these bonds covalent bonds.

Covalent bonds in gases

The atoms that make up common gases naturally occur as molecules. Hydrogen, oxygen, nitrogen, fluorine, and chlorine are

Some molecules, like oxygen, are very simple in appearance.

gases. Each molecule provides two atoms. For example, two oxygen atoms combined together make up one oxygen molecule. Covalent bonds hold them all together. These elements can only exist as molecules.

Ionic bonds

Sometimes, atoms link up with other atoms because they have extra electrons. Sometimes atoms link up with other atoms because they are missing electrons. We call these atoms ions. Ionic bonds hold the atoms together. Salt molecules are formed when sodium (Na) ions and chloride (Cl) ions bond together to make NaCl, or salt.

Sodium and chloride bond to make common table salt.

Types of ions. Scientists call an ion that is missing an electron or that has an extra proton a cation. An anion has an extra electron or is missing a proton.

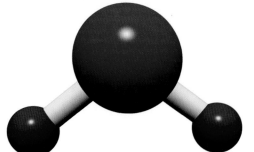

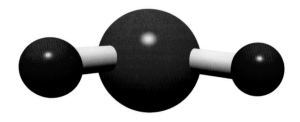

The two blue balls in each model represent hydrogen. The red balls represent oxygen. Each individual model represents one water molecule.

Hydrogen Bonds

Two atoms of hydrogen and one atom of oxygen form water. A covalent bond occurs when atoms share electrons with other atoms. Hydrogen bonds hold water together when water is a liquid. These bonds pull the hydrogen atoms of one water molecule close to the oxygen atoms of another water molecule. Hydrogen bonds are what give water such a high boiling point (212°F or 100°C).

equation (i-KWAY-zhuhn): a mathematical statement that one set of numbers or values is equal to another set of values or numbers

stable (STAY-buhl): firm and steady

Metallic Bonds

Metallic bonds hold together the atoms that form metal. Loosely attached electrons are in the outer shell of a metal atom. The electrons float around between the individual atoms in a sea of electrons. These electrons keep metal atoms in orderly rows. They fit together and flow easily in a metallic lattice. This allows heat and electricity to flow through the metal. Metallic bonds do not hold the atoms in place. When stretched or bent, atoms can move around. This movement is what enables metalworkers to make wire.

Wires conduct electricity. They enable us to talk on the phone, or recharge our iPods.

Timeline of the Atom Bomb	
1898	Marie Curie discovers radium and polonium.
1905	Albert Einstein develops a theory about the relationship between mass and energy.
1911	C.T.R. Wilson invents the cloud chamber.
1913	Radiation decay detector developed by Hans Geiger.
1925	First nuclear reaction captured by a cloud chamber photo.
1935	Arthur Dempster at the University of Chicago discovers uranium-235 isotope.
1939	Einstein and several other important scientists send a letter to the President of the United States, Franklin D. Roosevelt, detailing how Germany is developing and planning to use the first atom bomb.
1941	Japan attacks Pearl Harbor. The U.S. enters World War II.
1942	The Manhattan Project was established by the President to speed up research of the atom bomb. J. Robert Oppenheimer becomes the director in charge of its creation. Scientists all over the United States begin research and development.
July 1945	The first test of the atom bomb performed in New Mexico displays its unbelievable release of energy. It prompted many involved to sign petitions urging the United States not to use this weapon because of the destruction it can cause.
August 6, 1945	The first uranium bomb dropped on Hiroshima, Japan causes devastating destruction. Sixty-six thousand people die and more than 69,000 people are injured.
August 9, 1945	Three days later, a plutonium bomb devastates Nagasaki. More than 39,000 people died, and 25,000 were injured.
August 14, 1945	Japan offers to surrender. The surrender becomes official on September 2, 1945.
1945-Present	Many innocent people lost their lives in order for a war to end. Since that time, countries developed, threatened to use, and then disarmed themselves of nuclear weapons. It is the fervent wish of many that nuclear weapons become part of history and never used again.

Chemical Formulas

Scientists can describe a molecule or a compound with a chemical formula. A chemical formula is a written description of all the elements in a substance. Scientists sometimes write out chemical equations to figure out how different chemicals react with one another or to describe a reaction.

Common Molecules	Chemical Formula
Carbon Dioxide	CO_2
Ammonia	NH_3
Sugar	$C_6H_{12}O_6$
Rubbing Alcohol	C_3H_7OH

Molecular Formulas

Molecular formulas describe the exact number of atoms in a molecule. The tiny numbers to the bottom right of an element in a chemical formula stand for the number of atoms in that element. Water is a molecule made from two hydrogen atoms and one oxygen atom. H_2O is the molecular formula for water. The little 2 next to the H means that there are two hydrogen atoms. The O means that there is one atom of oxygen. Big numbers to the left of the atom stand for the number of molecules.

Water that is written as $5H_2O$ has 5 molecules of water.

One oxygen atom

Two hydrogen atoms

Structural Formulas

Structural formulas describe the arrangement of atoms within the molecules. A drawing of the formula shows the shape of the molecule.

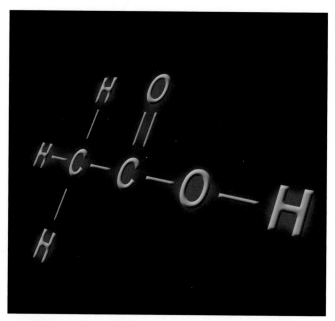

A structural formula displays the shape of the molecule similar to an actual model.

Matter

Matter is anything that takes up space and has mass. Atoms or parts of atoms form all matter. It is everything from the tiniest electron to the planets and stars.

Phases of Matter

Nearly all matter is a solid, a liquid, or a gas. These forms are called phases of matter.

Solids

Solids have a definite, or fixed, shape and volume. Their shape stays the same and they take up a certain amount of space. They are often very hard, or rigid. The molecules are usually locked in position. Molecules are made of at least two atoms. The colder a solid is, the less the molecules move.

The molecules of a solid will start to move as they are heated. Most metals in the periodic table are solids at room temperature. Silver bricks are a solid.

The desks, chairs, and books are solids in this classroom. They will hold their shape unless physically changed.

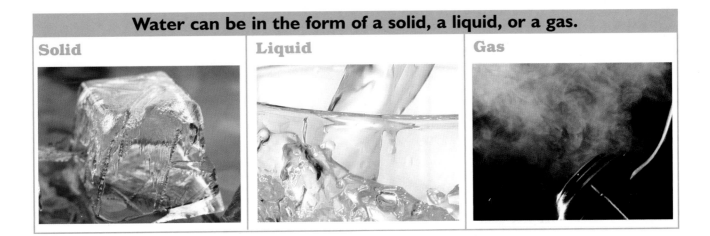

Water can be in the form of a solid, a liquid, or a gas.

Solid | Liquid | Gas

Liquids

Liquids have a fixed volume but not a fixed shape. The molecules in a liquid vibrate and move around each other easily. This means that they are fluid. Some liquids are thin, like water. It pours quickly. Other liquids are thick, like oil or syrup. They pour more slowly.

The gas in a popped bubble will not keep its shape.

Water is not as thick as oil. The oil will sink to the bottom of the water.

Gases

Gases have no fixed shape or volume. Gas fits into a container of almost any size. Gas molecules compress, or push together easily. Solid and liquid molecules do not function in the same way.

Some gases are lighter than air, like helium. An untied balloon filled with helium will float into the sky. Other gases are heavier than air, like carbon dioxide. You breathe out carbon dioxide with the air that leaves your lungs. A balloon filled with this mixture will sink to the floor.

Tropical rain forests take in carbon dioxide, a gas that we exhale, and changes it into clean air that we can breathe.

Atoms In Gases

The atoms in a gas can lose their electrons at really high temperatures. The result is a hot mixture of ions and electrons called plasma. This is another phase of matter. The flames of a fire are plasma. Lightning is plasma that forms when the air is electrically charged. Some scientists consider plasma to be a charged gas and not its own phase of matter.

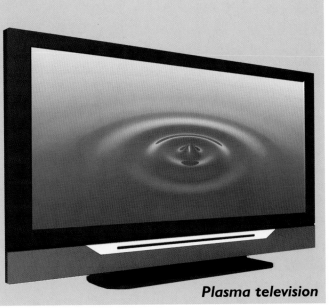

Plasma television

Properties of Matter

There are many ways to describe matter. Some things are either big or small. Other things might be hard or soft. An object might be light or heavy. A rock might be hot or cold. Some materials stretch into different shapes. Other materials mix easily with water. Still others float on water. All these descriptions tell you about the properties of matter.

Mass

Mass is the amount of matter in an object or substance. All forms of matter have mass. Solids, gases, and liquids have mass. The more neutrons and protons there are in an atom, the larger its mass will be. An atom of gold has 197 protons and neutrons. An atom of aluminum has only 27 protons and neutrons. This is why gold has a greater mass than aluminum.

Lava is a very hot liquid until it cools. Then, lava becomes a solid rock.

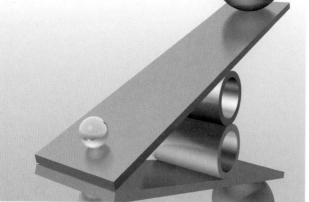

Comparing sizes of objects does not help us to determine mass. This scale shows us that gold has greater mass than aluminum.

Weight

Gravity pulls down on mass creating a force called weight. Mass and weight are proportional on the surface of the Earth. This means you double the weight of something if you double the amount of mass. In outer space, an object can be weightless, but still have the same mass. This is because gravity is not pulling on the object. Mass does not change, but weight depends on surrounding forces.

WORDS to know

mixture (MIKS-chur): something consisting of different things mixed together

properties (PROP-ur-tee): special qualities or characteristics of something

"I weigh 60 pounds."

"I weigh 10 pounds."

"My weight changed, but my mass didn't change. My body still contains all the same stuff it contained when I was on Earth."

Planet	Weight (lb)	Weight (kg)
Mercury	33	15
Venus	79	36
Mars	33	15
Jupiter	207	94
Saturn	79	36
Uranus	77	35
Neptune	97	44

The pull of gravity is different on each of the planets in our solar system. If you weighed 88 lbs (40 kg) on Earth, the table will show you how much you would weigh on the other planets. Your mass would still stay the same.

Volume

Another way to describe the amount of something is its volume. Volume is the amount of space taken up by matter. An object can have a large mass but take up only a small amount of volume. An object can also have a small mass but take up a lot of volume.

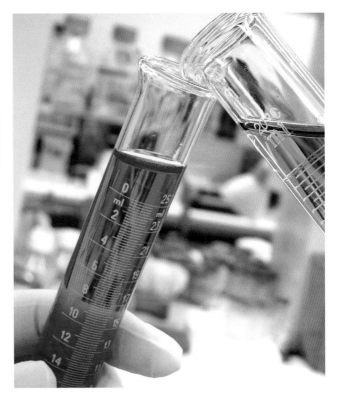

Scientists measure liquid volume in graduated cylinders that are marked with the units milliliter and liter.

The cotton candy's volume is greater than the golf ball. The golf ball's mass is greater than the cotton candy.

Density

Density is the amount of mass for a certain volume. A block of iron is heavier than a block of wood that has the same size or volume. Iron is more dense than wood. Gases are not as dense as solids and liquids. Different gases have different densities. Hydrogen and helium are not as dense as oxygen and nitrogen. This is why a helium balloon floats up into the air.

These rocks are denser than the liquid.

A solid that is not as dense as a liquid will float on it. A denser solid will sink in it. The buoyancy of an object describes how well it floats on top of a liquid. Cork floats because it is not as dense as water. A boat can float because its shape allows it to contain a lot of air. The air in the boat is less dense than the water beneath the boat. The boat will sink if it fills up with too much water.

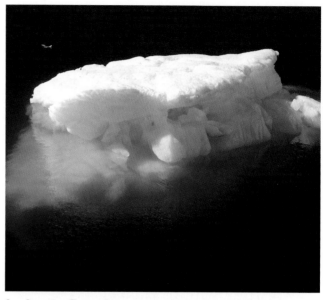

Icebergs float because they are slightly less dense than water. Most of the iceberg is below the surface of the water.

Find out more
Water has the density of 1.0 g/cm². Saturn's density is .69 g/cm². If you were to go to Saturn and return with a chunk of the planet, you could throw it in a body of water and watch it float!

Saturn

Conductors of Heat

Heat can be conducted, or passed, through many types of matter. Metals are very good conductors of heat. The energy in heat conducts from one end of a piece of metal to the other end. This is why a metal spoon gets hot when only one end is touching the source of the heat.

The prongs of this plug will conduct electricity to the wires in the cord. The wires will conduct the electricity to the appliance. The plastic covering around the wires allows us to be able to hold the cord without burning our hands.

Liquids can also be good conductors of electricity. This is why it is a bad idea to use an electric device near water. For example, never use a hair dryer near a bathtub filled with water.

The glowing end of this metal rod shows us its intense heat. Eventually, the heat will transfer along the rod to the other end.

Conductors of Electricity

Metals are also good conductors of electricity. Electrons flow easily between the atoms of a metal. An electrical current at one end of a metal wire quickly passes through to the other end.

Get out of a pool immediately if you hear thunder or see lightning!

Semiconductors. Other elements can also be good conductors of electricity. Semiconductors can conduct electricity when they are heated. Silicon, when mixed with other elements, is a very good semiconductor.

Most solid materials are poor conductors of electricity. Wood, plastic, and glass are electrical insulators. The plastic covering on wires acts as an insulator. The plastic prevents wires from touching each other and causing electrical problems.

Semiconductors enable us to use many everyday items, such as a cell phone.

insulator (IN-suh-late-ur): a covering which prevents heat or electricity from escaping

Some Metals Are Liquids

Most people think of metals as hard and strong. Some metals are actually liquids! Mercury is the only metal that is a complete liquid. This happens at room temperature. Thermometers and electrical switches use mercury. Other metals become liquids at higher temperatures.

Mercury is very poisonous. If a thermometer drops and breaks, stay away from the mercury and wait for an adult to help you.

Elasticity

Rubber bands have elasticity. They will snap back into their original shape if you stretch them and then let go. Other things made out of rubber show this same elastic property. A balloon will return to its original shape if you let the air out of it.

Rubber bands have elasticity. They will snap back to their original shape if you stretch them and let go.

Elastic Limit. Other materials are not as elastic. Metal springs bounce back into shape after being stretched or compressed. An overstretched spring will not return to its exact original shape. The point to which you can stretch a material and still have it bounce back is called the elastic limit. Almost all materials have at least a little bit of elasticity.

When you chew gum, you are really chewing plastic and rubber with a little bit of flavoring. Gum is not as elastic as a rubber band.

Solubility

PROJECTS volume 10 5.2

Solubility is the ability to dissolve. A substance dissolves and distributes evenly into another substance. The dissolved substance may be difficult to detect. Sugar dissolves in hot tea. After stirring, it is difficult to see the sugar.

Sugar dissolves easily in a hot cup of coffee.

Changes in Solubility. Solids, liquids, and gases dissolve into liquids. They form a solution. A solution is a mixture of more than one thing. The solubility of solids and liquids can change. This can happen when the temperature changes. Solubility will increase as the temperature increases. This means that more liquids or solids dissolve at higher temperatures. It will also increase as pressure is increased. The solution is saturated when no more of a substance can be dissolved into it.

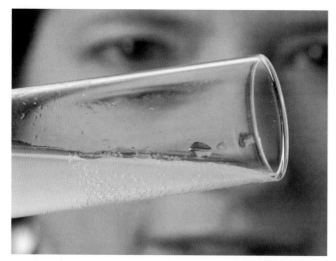

This water is saturated. You can clearly see the crystals of salt that will not dissolve.

Changes in Matter

Boiling Point

The boiling point of water changes depending on your elevation. The boiling point of water at the highest point in the Rocky Mountains is 194°F (90°C).

Some phases of matter can change into other phases. This can happen when the conditions are right. A liquid heated enough will change into a gas. Scientists call the temperature at which this begins the boiling point. The boiling point of a liquid will increase as the pressure is increased. At sea level, water boils at 212°F (100°C). Water boils at a lower temperature at higher altitudes. This is because there is less air pressure pushing against the water.

Evaporation

Water is the most common liquid on the planet. It changes into a gas called water vapor as it is heated. Water is absorbed into the atmosphere through a process called evaporation.

The water in this puddle will not really disappear. It will evaporate back into the atmosphere.

Condensation

Water vapor that cools will turn back into a liquid. Cold metal or glass can help speed up this process. Little drops of water build up on a cold surface as the molecules in the water vapor begin to move more slowly. Condensation is the buildup of little drops of water.

Carbon dioxide freezes at -109° F (-78° C), turning it into dry ice. Dry ice gives the appearance of fog or smoke when exposed to warmer temperatures.

The cold iced tea caused condensation to form on the outside of this glass.

Melting Point

Heated enough, a solid will melt into a liquid. The melting point is the temperature at which a solid begins melting. Nearly all metals are solids at room temperature. Hard rocks will melt deep below the surface of the Earth. This is because of high temperatures. Ice cream is solid as long as it is kept cold. It becomes a liquid as it melts.

Sublimation

Sublimation occurs when certain solids turn directly into gas. A gas will form if the molecules of a solid move fast enough. Dry ice is frozen carbon dioxide. Dry ice does not change into a liquid before changing into a gas.

Ice cream does not remain a solid for long if left out in the Sun.

Freezing Point

The freezing point of a liquid is the temperature at which it becomes a solid. Water will freeze at 0° Celsius or 32° Fahrenheit.

Many children are elated when a liquid reaches the freezing point!

Robert Boyle

Getting to know... Robert Boyle, the founder of chemistry, was born in Ireland in 1627. His father was one of the richest men in the country of Great Britain. Boyle went to the best schools. He had the money to set up laboratories for his work in science.

Boyle thought about science in a new way. He believed in testing theories. He designed experiments for other scientists to repeat. He wrote down all of his results. He was the first to suggest that certain kinds of matter share similar chemical properties. He noted the difference between atoms and elements.

Compounds, Acids and Bases, Mixtures, and Solutions

Every material is made of either a pure substance or a combination of substances. A substance is pure if it contains only one type of element. An element is a substance made up of all of the same type of atoms. Oxygen is a pure substance. It only contains oxygen atoms. Elements combine in several ways. Some of these combinations will always stay together while others separate.

This steel container is rusting. A chemical reaction occurs when the iron from the can meets the oxygen in the air.

Compounds

A compound is a combination of two or more elements. These elements exist in the compound in fixed amounts. A chemical reaction occurs during the formation of a compound. The chemical reaction may produce light or heat. It might also produce some other kind of change. Compounds often look very different from the elements from which they came. The elements that make up the compound lose their identity. There is only one way to separate the elements that make a compound. This is with another chemical reaction.

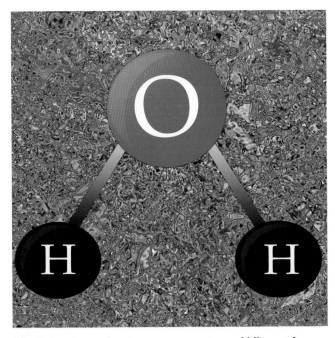

Hydrogen and oxygen are gases. When they form a compound, their characteristics are very different. Combined, they become a liquid, water.

Simple Compounds

Simple compounds are different kinds of combined elements. They combine chemically. Water is the most common compound. It is made of 2 parts of hydrogen (H) and 1 part of oxygen (O). Sugar, alcohol, baking soda, and acids are all different types of compounds. Millions of different compounds exist in nature. Scientists have the ability to form many compounds in laboratories.

Getting to know... Sir Humphry Davy

Humphry Davy was born in England in 1778. At sixteen, he worked for a surgeon. At first, Davy wanted to be a doctor. Then he became interested in chemistry. He began to create his own experiments.

Davy suggested that compounds break down into elements. This happens when electricity passes through them. Scientists call this electrolysis. Davy used electrolysis to separate many elements.

He also used it to study a substance called muriatic acid. We now call this hydrochloric acid. Some people thought that all acids contain oxygen. Davy found that muriatic acid has hydrogen and chlorine but no oxygen. He realized that all acids contain hydrogen.

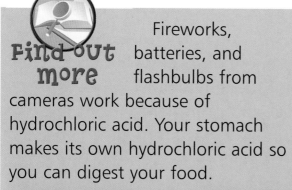

Find out more

Fireworks, batteries, and flashbulbs from cameras work because of hydrochloric acid. Your stomach makes its own hydrochloric acid so you can digest your food.

Battery acid is very strong. Never touch or use a leaky battery.

Acids and Bases

PROJECTS
volume 10
5.3

Acids

An acid is a substance. It gives up hydrogen ions in solutions containing water. Some acids are weak. They contain fewer hydrogen ions. Other acids are strong. They contain more hydrogen ions.

Inorganic Acids

Acids made from minerals are inorganic acids or mineral acids. Minerals are things found in nature. They are not plants or animals. These acids, often used to make commercial products, are liquids. Sulfuric acid is one of the most often used chemicals in the United States. We use it to make gasoline, plastics, and many other products. Some gardeners use fertilizer made from nitric acid and phosphoric acid.

Fertilizers help gardens grow and stay beautiful.

Organic Acids

Humans make an acid in their stomachs called hydrochloric acid. Hydrochloric acid helps digest, or break down, food. Mucus, a thick substance inside the stomach, protects it from hydrochloric acid. Hydrochloric acid can eat through the lining of the stomach. This happens when there is not enough mucus to protect it. People can get a hole in their stomachs called an ulcer.

Some acids are in the foods that people eat. A food that tastes sour probably contains citric acid. Lemons, oranges, and grapefruits all contain citric acid.

Citric acid crystallized from lemon juice is used in everything from shampoo to photography.

Sometimes people get sore muscles from a buildup of lactic acid in their muscles. Milk that spoils also makes lactic acid.

Butter that goes bad makes butyric acid. Vinegar contains an acid called acetic acid. We call all of these acids organic acids because they occur naturally.

Bases

The opposite of an acid is a base. Bases cancel out, or neutralize, an acid. We call bases dissolved in water alkalis. Bases are everywhere.

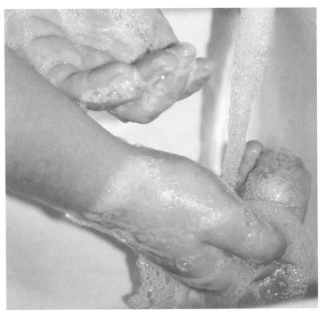

Soap is a common base we use everyday.

Strong Bases. Sodium hydroxide is a strong base used to make soap and other cleaning agents. Strong alkalis are often caustic. This means that they can burn skin. They can also dissolve some substances. Some alkalis are even poisonous.

Weak Bases. Ammonia, or ammonium hydroxide, is a weak alkali base used in many cleaning and disinfecting products. Foods that contain weak alkalis often taste bitter. So do some things that are not edible. Soap bubbles taste bitter because of the alkalis in them.

Unsweetened chocolate contains alkalis which causes it to taste bitter.

pH

People can tell how strong an acid or a base is. They find this by measuring its pH. Acidity is how strong an acid is. Alkalinity is how strong a base is.

The symbol pH stands for "power of hydrogen." It is measured on a scale from 1 to 14. A strong acid might have a pH of 1. Sulfuric acid and hydrochloric acid have a low pH. They can burn through clothes and skin. At the other end of the scale are bases. A pH of 14 means that the solution is a strong base. Strong bases are also dangerous. A neutral solution is neither an acid nor a base. A neutral solution has a pH of 7.

There are many ways to determine the pH of something. Use litmus paper to see if a liquid is an acid or a base. The paper turns red if dipped in an acid. The paper turns blue if dipped in a base. Scientists can measure pH accurately by using a special machine called a pH meter.

It is very important to know what the pH of a substance is. A person can die if the pH of the blood changes even a little. Doctors must make sure that any solutions used to help people are neutral.

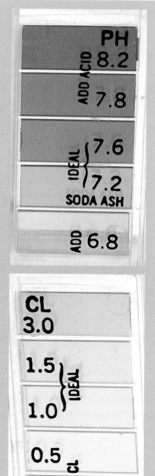

Mixtures

Many things are combinations of substances. A mixture is matter made up of different parts. The parts have different properties. The parts of a mixture can be present in any amount or proportion. No chemical reaction occurs in a mixture. There is no flash of light or heat. Heterogeneous mixtures look like they have different parts. The parts that make up a mixture keep their identities. Heterogeneous mixtures easily separate.

A salad is an example of a heterogeneous mixture.

Making and Separating Mixtures

There are many ways to mix and separate a mixture. Simply dump two materials together to make a mixture. Cement is a mixture made by pouring water into a special

kind of sand. Mud is a mixture of dirt and water.

Cement is a mixture used for sidewalks and streets. There are four essential ingredients in cement: calcium, silicon, aluminum, and iron.

Sometimes, mixtures form over a very long period of time. Granite is a type of rock that is actually a mixture of three other kinds of rock. It is made of quartz, feldspar, and mica rock.

It can take millions of years for granite to form.

Mixtures used in preparing food, such as Italian salad dressing, are often a mixture of oil, vinegar, and spices. The dressing will separate into three layers if you let it sit long enough.

Shake a bottle of salad dressing before you use it. The greater the density of the liquid, the more it will separate and sink.

Solutions

Many types of mixtures do not seem like mixtures at all. They often look like only one substance when they are actually two or more. We call these mixtures solutions, or homogeneous mixtures.

Solids combined with liquids form some solutions. A mixture of sugar and water can make a solution called sugar water. The sugar disappears, or dissolves into the water. Sugar water tastes sweet even though the sugar is dissolved. When the water evaporates, the sugar remains. Then the water will have changed into a gas and you will only be able to see the sugar.

Hot chocolate is a delicious solution on a cold winter day.

Find out more

Air

Do you wonder what is in the air that you breathe? Air is actually a mixture of gases. It is mostly a solution of nitrogen and oxygen gases. There are other gases in air such as carbon dioxide and water vapor. Other gases are in the air because of natural and human activity.

Volcanos send sulfur dioxide and carbon monoxide into the air. Forest fires also add carbon monoxide. Tiny living creatures remove some of these poisonous gases from the air. Human activity adds many different gases into

Making and Separating Solutions

Two liquids combined form a solution. Alcohol dissolved into water is a solution. Evaporation separates the solution. Alcohol will evaporate first. This is because it has a lower boiling point than water.

Gold and silver become liquids if they become hot enough. Liquid gold and silver separate when heated. The gold will settle to the bottom because it is heavier than silver.

A gas and a liquid can also make a solution. Carbon dioxide mixed with water makes a solution called soda water. When soda water separates, carbon dioxide bubbles rise out of the liquid. Pressure releases from the can or bottle of soda.

carbon dioxide

the air. Exhaust from cars and factories create harmful carbon monoxide. Smog forms when sunlight reacts with carbon monoxide and other gases in the air. High levels of smog can cause health problems in humans.

Humans and animals change the air around them. They do this when they breathe. They breathe in the oxygen and nitrogen. They breathe out a new mixture of air containing carbon dioxide. Plants use carbon dioxide during the process of making food called photosynthesis. One product of photosynthesis is oxygen.

We can help our environment and ourselves by reducing the number of cars on the road. We should walk, ride a bike, take a train, take a bus, or carpool whenever possible.

Reactions

Chemical Reactions

A chemical reaction occurs when chemicals combine and change. Reactions are constantly taking place. Many occur in nature. Some reactions take place inside animals and plants. The food that humans and other animals eat digests as a series of chemical reactions. Photosynthesis is a series of chemical reactions in plants. This is how plants make food.

Photosynthesis, a chemical reaction powered by the Sun, changes carbon dioxide and water into oxygen and sugar.

Other chemical reactions caused by humans take place every day in factories. Chemical reactions take place above the surface of the Earth. Some of these reactions protect the Earth from harmful things. Chemical reactions make all life possible.

Combining Chemicals

Reactants and Products. There are many different ways that chemicals combine, or react. A chemical reaction occurs when one substance is broken apart and then put together as a new substance. Reactants are the starting substances. Scientists call the new substances products. Atoms and molecules rearrange during a chemical reaction, but do not disappear or change. Reactions speed up when special chemicals are used. Reactions also release some form of energy.

The head of a match contains sulfur, glass powder, and an oxidizing agent. Friction from striking the match creates enough heat to cause a chemical reaction, and fire.

Making and Breaking Bonds

All chemical reactions involve making and breaking bonds between atoms. Every time a chemical reaction takes place, chemical bonds pull apart and come back together. Energy is required for bonds to break. This energy can take many forms. Some chemical reactions take place when there is heat or light. Other reactions need electricity to get started.

Scientists use this device to measure the heat of reactions. Scientists like you can also use a styrofoam cup and get similar results!

Mass

All chemical reactions conserve mass. This means that the amount of atoms at the beginning of a reaction is the same as the amount of atoms at the end of a reaction. The atoms just move places. The number of atoms is the same on both sides of a chemical equation.

Catalysts

A catalyst is a chemical that changes the speed of a reaction, but does not change in the reaction. Some catalysts are a single substance. Other catalysts are a combination of many substances. Catalysts do not start reactions. Most catalysts speed up reactions. Inhibitors are catalysts that slow down reactions. Some inhibitors cause other catalysts to stop working.

Catalysts help do many different things. They can allow reactions to happen at lower temperatures. Some catalysts help bring reactants close together. In manufacturing, they help to produce gasoline, rubber, and medicine. Catalysts remain at the end of a reaction, making them reusable. This helps save companies money.

Companies keep their catalysts a secret. If two companies are producing the same product and one has a better catalyst, that company will be more successful. The company can produce more of that product faster and for a cheaper price.

Helpful Catalysts

Enzymes are catalysts made by living cells. They help speed up chemical reactions in the human body. Each enzyme will work in only one type of reaction. Enzymes help digest food in the body. They help do this in only a few hours. Digestion would take several weeks without enzymes.

Thankfully, enzymes speed up the digestion process!

Harmful Catalysts

Catalysts in the Earth's atmosphere are causing troubles. They are causing the ozone layer to break down. Ozone protects the Earth from harmful ultraviolet rays from the Sun. Chlorine is a catalyst in the upper atmosphere. The chlorine comes from chlorofluorocarbons, or CFCs, released into the atmosphere. Chlorine allows ozone to break down into oxygen. The chlorine remains and keeps destroying ozone. This has caused a hole in the ozone layer. Governments around the world have banned the production of CFCs. This hole in the ozone now appears to be shrinking. We must continue to protect the ozone layer by reducing pollution around the world. Some scientists believe the ozone layer could return to normal levels by 2075.

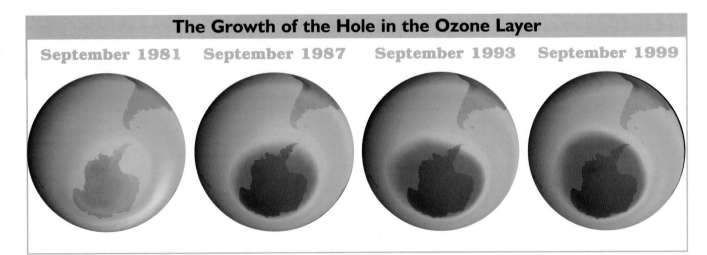

The Growth of the Hole in the Ozone Layer

September 1981   September 1987   September 1993   September 1999

Oxidation and Reduction

Whenever a molecule takes up oxygen, something else has to give up oxygen. An oxidized substance combines with oxygen or loses hydrogen. We call the substance that loses oxygen or gains hydrogen reduced. Oxidation and reduction always go together. They can also take place between the electrons of two atoms. Scientists call this an electron transfer. Photsynthesis occurs because of electron transfers. Atoms that lose electrons oxidize. Atoms that gain electrons reduce.

Find out more

Some Metals Turn to Dust

Air and water can eat away iron and steel! Oxygen binds to iron molecules to make iron oxide. Layer by layer, the metal changes to a red powder called rust. When painted, rusting slows on cars, bicycles, and tricycles.

Food

Many different kinds of chemical processes use oxidation and reduction. Food that gets old oxidizes and goes bad. Keeping food refrigerated slows down the rate of oxidation. Humans and animals also rely on this reaction. The food people and animals eat is oxidized in the cells. This helps give the body energy.

Cows graze all day to give them energy and help their bodies make milk.

Germs

A weak solution of hydrogen peroxide is a common reducing agent. The chemical formula for hydrogen peroxide is H_2O_2. When reduced, it becomes water and oxygen. A solution of hydrogen peroxide kills germs. Bleach sometimes contains stronger solutions of hydrogen peroxide. Bleaching is a process that removes color from cotton and wool. Bleach makes clothes whiter. It also kills germs.

Bleach whitened these socks and removed germs and bacteria.

Fires

Fires are common oxidation reactions. Fire consumes a lot of oxygen. This is because the material that is burning oxidizes at a very fast rate. Flames erupt because the reaction energy is so intense. Fires need oxygen, heat, and fuel. Materials cannot burn when there is no oxygen.

Water takes heat from fire when turning into steam. It also cuts the supply of oxygen to the fire so it will go out more quickly.

Combustion

Combustion is a form of burning. Combustion helps to drive motors, propel airplanes, and launch rockets. Rockets in outer space carry oxygen in their fuel. They need the oxygen for combustion to take place. Gasoline engines are sometimes called combustion engines. Gasoline burns inside the engine. The oxidation reaction releases energy that makes the car move.

On March 16, 1926, Dr. Robert Goddard launched the first rocket into the atmosphere. Today, rockets launched into outer space are a common occurrence.

Antoine-Laurent Lavoisier

Getting to know...

Antoine-Laurent Lavoisier was born in France in 1743. His father and grandfather were lawyers, so he became a lawyer too. However, Lavoisier was more interested in science.

Lavoisier wanted to make chemistry a separate science. He began to experiment with combustion. Some scientists believed that burning released a material called phlogiston. Lavoisier discovered that phlogiston does not exist. He also showed that air and water are compounds. He proved that many elements occur in different phases, as solids, liquids, or gases. Lavoisier came up with the names "oxygen" and "hydrogen."

Releasing Energy

Exothermic Reactions

The temperature of chemicals changes as they react with each other. Heat releases or is absorbed into the compound during a chemical reaction. The compound becomes warm or hot when heat releases. Scientists call this an exothermic reaction. Most of the chemical reactions that occur in nature are slow exothermic reactions. They take place so slowly that it is difficult to notice the release of heat. Exothermic reactions are often easy to see when fuels burn. Energy releases from oxidation that occurs while fuel is burning. This is why fires are so hot.

Endothermic Reactions

Reacting chemicals become cooler when heat is absorbed. Scientists call this an endothermic reaction. Photosynthesis is one of the few natural endothermic reactions. Photosynthesis occurs when plants convert or change sunlight, carbon dioxide, and water into oxygen and food. Plants actually get a little bit cooler during photosynthesis.

Cold packs, used by doctors and athletes, lower the temperature of an injury. A cold pack contains two chemicals. The chemicals react with each other when they are mixed. The endothermic reaction absorbs heat from the injured part of the body. It helps to cool the body down.

An exothermic reaction occurs when vinegar removes the coating from a steel wool pad. When the steel meets oxygen, oxidation occurs, releasing heat.

Athletes use cold packs that do not have to be frozen. To get the pack to be cold, the athlete smashes the pack on a hard surface. The chemicals inside the pack mix together, causing them to become very cold.

Explosions

Exothermic Reactions

A chemical reaction might blow up, or explode. This happens when it releases a lot of energy all at once. Explosions are very fast exothermic reactions. These reactions can happen in many different ways.

an explosive oxidation. Gases like hydrogen and propane explode if they mix with oxygen and then encounter a flame. Some liquids can explode if they become a gas, called vapor. Vapors allow molecules to bond with oxygen much more easily. Gasoline vapors can explode if a spark ignites gasoline fumes.

Huge explosions occur under unsafe conditions.

We create small explosions when we light a gas grill.

Explosive Oxidation

Explosions on the Earth often take place when there are combustible materials around. These materials bond easily with oxygen. They can catch on fire. Sometimes, we call this reaction

Other explosions do not need oxygen from the air. Explosive materials often contain chemicals that provide their own oxygen. Gunpowder is a mixture of potassium nitrate, sulfur and other chemicals. Potassium nitrate (KNO_3) contains lots of oxygen. Gunpowder burns by getting its oxygen from potassium nitrate, not the air. Dynamite is an explosive made from tightly packed gunpowder. When dynamite ignites, it makes a very powerful explosion. Fireworks also use various amounts of gunpowder and other chemicals. These mixtures make the variety of colors and explosions seen in fireworks displays.

Joseph Black

Getting to know... Joseph Black was born in 1728 in France. His father was from the country of Ireland. He sent Black there for his education. Black then went to college in the country of Scotland. He lived there the rest of his life.

Black, known for his study of heat, showed that different substances need more or less heating time to reach the same temperature. He also noticed that phase changes (solid, liquid, gas) gain or lose heat.

The First Fireworks

Find out more More than 2,000 years ago, a Chinese cook accidentally combined potassium nitrate, sulfur, and charcoal. The combination ignited and exploded, creating the first firecracker. The Chinese explode the "huo-yao," or fire chemicals, during celebrations such as religious holidays and weddings. Many believed that the loud noise scared away evil spirits. Today, people around the world use firecrackers as symbols of joy during holidays and events.

Find out more

Fermentation

Fruit starts to smell funny as it gets too ripe. There is a change going on inside the rotting fruit. It is a chemical reaction. Small organisms or living things, called microbes change the sugars in the fruit. They change them into carbon dioxide and either water or alcohol. Scientists call this chemical process fermentation.

Fermentation without the presence of oxygen produces alcohol and carbon dioxide. Sugar is broken down into alcohol and carbon dioxide. This happens with the help of an enzyme from the microbes. The enzyme makes a chemical reaction happen.

Humans use fermentation to make other kinds of foods and medicines. Bread would not exist without yeast. Yeast is a microbe, or living thing. Yeast converts the sugars in wheat grains into carbon dioxide and water. The gas causes the bread to rise and to look like a sponge. The yeast dies as the bread is cooked. Humans also use a fermentation process to make penicillin and other medicines.

Many types of fermented foods can make people sick. E. coli are bacteria that cause raw meat to ferment. Eating undercooked meat with E. coli in it can make a person very ill.

Yeast   *Dough rising*   *Bread*

Archeologists discovered that people started to bake bread using yeast in 4,000 B.C. Before that, bread was usually flat.

People Who Study Chemistry

Hundreds of years ago, people called alchemists used chemical reactions. They used them to make medicines and combine metals. Some of them thought they could create gold from other metals. Some of them thought they could make people live forever. Unfortunately, they were wrong. Today, we know a lot more about how things really work.

Types of Chemists

Chemistry is the study of how chemicals react with one another and the products they make.
Chemists are people who study chemistry. There are many different kinds of chemists.

Chemistry makes life possible. Everything from the tiniest atoms, to the blood in our bodies, to the shoes on our feet is the result of chemical reactions. People will keep learning about chemistry and how it affects our lives.

Gerhard Ertl

Getting to know... In 1901, the first Nobel prizes, named for Alfred Nobel, a wealthy industrialist, recognized achievers in the fields of literature, chemistry, medicine, physics, and peace. Every year, outstanding people from all over the world, continue to receive this prestigious award.

On October 10, 2007, Gerhard Ertl of Germany received an amazing 71st birthday present, the Nobel Prize in Chemistry. His research in answering questions such as why iron rusts, how fuel cells function, and how catalysts work, helps to explain the reasons behind Earth's damaged ozone layer. Ertl's prize includes a gold medal, a diploma, and 10 million krona (Swedish) or about $1.5 million (U.S.).

Chemistry is used to make video games!

THERE ARE MANY PROFESSIONS THAT USE CHEMISTRY

Profession		What They Involve
Analytic chemists	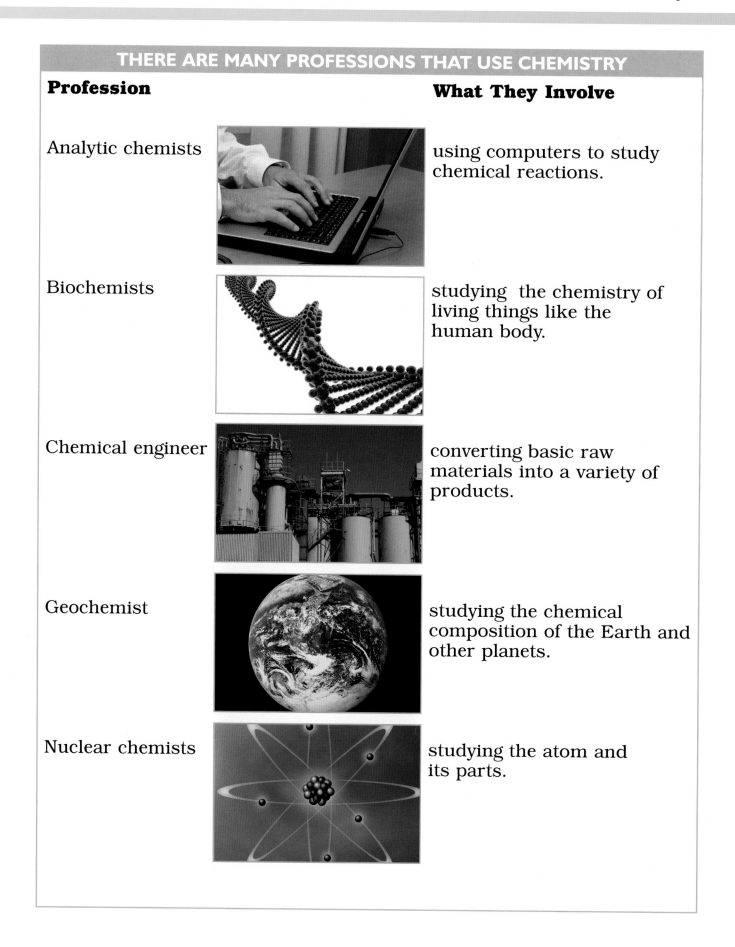	using computers to study chemical reactions.
Biochemists		studying the chemistry of living things like the human body.
Chemical engineer		converting basic raw materials into a variety of products.
Geochemist		studying the chemical composition of the Earth and other planets.
Nuclear chemists		studying the atom and its parts.

Profession		What They Involve
Organic chemists	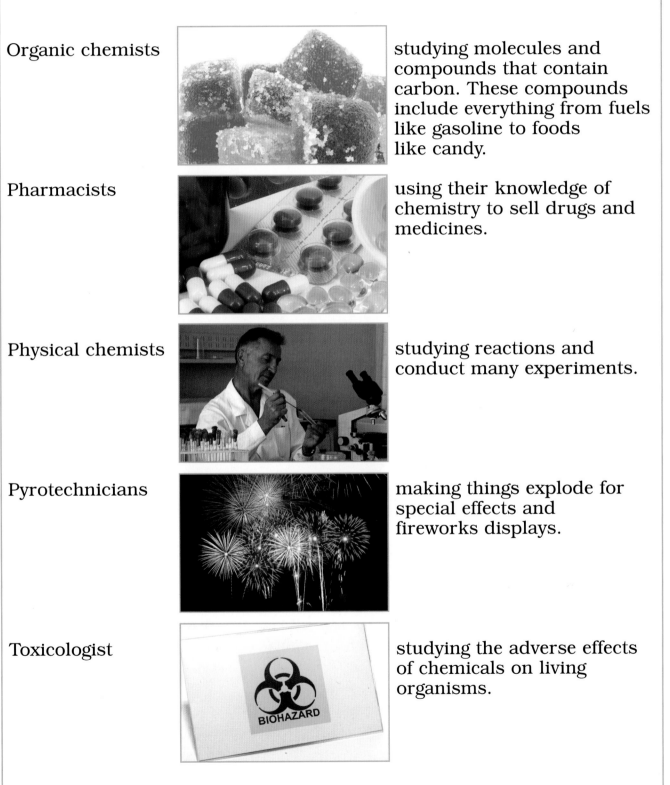	studying molecules and compounds that contain carbon. These compounds include everything from fuels like gasoline to foods like candy.
Pharmacists		using their knowledge of chemistry to sell drugs and medicines.
Physical chemists		studying reactions and conduct many experiments.
Pyrotechnicians		making things explode for special effects and fireworks displays.
Toxicologist		studying the adverse effects of chemicals on living organisms.

Types of Chemists

We do not hear much about women in science, but without their contributions, the world would be a very different place. This timeline highlights a few of the thousands of women who have contributed enormously to the study of chemistry.

Women In Chemistry	
1842-1911	Ellen Swallow Richards: First female to study at MIT. She pioneered the study of Home Economics.
1867-1934	Marie Curie: Discovered radium.
1896-1957	Gerty Cori: Her work in biochemistry made a great impact on research in diabetes. She was the first American woman to win the Nobel Prize in science.
1897-1956	Irene Joliot Curie: Won a Nobel Prize for chemistry for her work with radioactive elements.
1910-1994	Dorothy Crowfoot Hodgkin: Won the 1964 Nobel Prize in chemistry for her work on vitamin B12.
1920-2007	Katsuko Saruhashi conducted some of the first radioactive research showing how the effects of fallout can impact the entire Earth, not just the immediate area. She also studied acid rain and its effects.

acid(s)   40, 41, 42, 43, 44, 62
air   19, 21, 30, 31, 34, 36, 38, 40, 46,
    47, 52, 54, 56, 57
alcohol   28, 41, 47, 58
alkali metals   18
alkalis   43, 44
ammonia   28, 44
anion   25
atom bomb   23, 27
atomic mass   23, 27
atomic number   15, 17, 18, 20, 21
atom(s)   11, 12, 13, 14, 19, 20, 24, 25,
    26, 28, 29, 31, 35, 40, 48, 49, 52, 59
balloon   15, 30, 34, 36
base(s)   40, 42, 43, 44
Black, Joseph   57
bleach   53
Bohr, Niels   13
bond(s)   18, 25, 26, 49, 56
cancer   21, 22, 23
carbon   14, 16, 19, 20, 21, 22, 61
carbon dioxide   28, 30, 39, 46, 47, 48,
    55, 58
catalyst(s)   49, 50, 51, 59
cation   25
Celsius scale   10
centimeter   8
CFCs   51
changes in matter   38
chemical formula(s)   28, 53
chemical reaction(s)   4, 40, 41, 45, 48,
    49, 51, 55, 56, 58, 59, 60
chemistry   4, 5, 7, 23, 40, 41, 54, 59,
    60, 61, 62
Chernobyl   23
citric acid   43
combustion   54
compound(s)   28, 40, 41, 54, 55, 61
condensation   39
conductors   35, 36
Cori, Gerty   62
covalent bond(s)   25, 26
Curie, Irene Joliot   62
Curie, Marie   23, 27, 62
Curie, Pierre   23
Davy, Sir Humphry   41

density   34, 46
Earth   9, 19, 20, 32, 33, 39, 48, 51,
    56, 59, 60, 62
elasticity   36, 37
electricity   14, 26, 35, 36, 41, 49
electrolysis   41
electron microscope   11
electron shell   11, 12, 18
electron(s)   11, 12, 13, 15, 17, 18, 21,
    25, 26, 29, 31, 35, 52
element(s)   11, 14, 15, 16, 17, 18, 20,
    22, 23, 24, 25, 28, 36, 40, 41, 54, 62
endothermic   55
energy   7, 13, 27, 35, 48, 53, 54, 55,
    56
enzyme(s)   4, 51, 58
equation   26, 28, 49
Ertl, Gerhard   59
evaporation   38, 47
exothermic   55, 56
experiment(s)   5, 6, 7, 40, 41, 54, 61
explosion(s)   23, 56, 57
fermentation   58
fire   31, 46, 48, 53, 55, 56, 57
food   4, 21, 22, 42, 43, 44, 46, 47, 48,
    51, 53, 55, 58, 61
formula(s)   28, 53
freezing point   40
gas(es)   7, 14, 18, 25, 29, 30, 31, 34,
    37, 38, 39, 41, 42, 46, 47, 49, 54, 56,
    57, 58, 61
Geiger counter   22
gluons   12
gold   14, 16, 31, 32, 47, 59
gravity   9, 18, 33, 32
group   17, 18, 19
gunpowder   56, 57
heat   7, 10, 14, 26, 29, 35, 36, 38, 39,
    41, 45, 47, 48, 49, 53, 55, 57
helium   15, 16, 18, 25, 30, 34
Hiroshima   23, 27
Hodgkin, Dorothy Crowfoot   62
hydrochloric acid   41, 42, 43, 44
hydrogen   15, 16, 18, 19, 20, 25, 26,
    28, 34, 41, 42, 44, 52, 53, 54, 56
hydrogen bonds   26

hydrogen peroxide   53
hypothesis   6, 7
inhibitors   49
insulators   36
ionic bonds   25
ions   25, 31, 42
isotopes   20, 21, 22, 27
Kelvin scale   10
kilogram   9
kilometer   8
laboratory   6, 21
lactic acid   43
Lavoisier, Antoine-Laurent   54
liquids   14, 26, 29, 30, 31, 33, 34, 35,
   36, 38, 39, 40, 41, 42, 44, 46, 47, 54,
   56, 57
litmus paper   44
mass   9, 15, 20, 21, 27, 31, 32, 33, 34,
   49
mass spectrometer   20
matter   9, 11, 20, 29, 31, 33, 35, 38,
   40, 45
measurement   8, 9, 10, 15, 21
melting point   39
Mendeleyev, Dmitry   19
mercury   33, 36
metallic bonds   26
metal(s)   14, 18, 29, 35, 36, 39, 52, 59
meter   8, 44
metric system   8, 10
milligram   9
mixtures   20, 40, 45, 46, 57
molecular formula   28
molecules   24, 25, 28, 29, 30, 39, 48,
   52, 56, 61
neutron(s)   11, 12, 15, 20, 21, 24, 31
noble gases   18, 25
nonmetals   14
nucleus   11, 12, 13, 15, 20, 21
observation   5, 6, 7
oxidation   52, 53, 54, 55, 56
oxygen   14, 15, 16, 19, 20, 25, 26, 28,
   34, 40, 41, 46, 47, 48, 51, 52, 53, 54,
   55, 56, 57, 58
ozone   51, 59
particle accelerators   13

period   17, 18, 45
Periodic Table   15, 16, 17, 18, 19, 29
pH   44
phases of matter   29, 38
plasma   31
properties of matter   31
protons   11, 12, 15, 17, 18, 20, 21, 24,
   25, 31
radiation   21, 22, 23, 27
radioactive decay   21
radioactive isotopes   21, 22
radioactivity   22, 23
reactants   48, 49
reactions   4, 48, 49, 51, 53, 55, 56, 59,
   61, 60
reduction   52, 53
Richards, Ellen Swallow   62
rockets   4, 54
rubber   4, 37, 36, 49
salt   25, 38
Saruhashi, Katsuko   62
scale   9, 10, 32, 44
scientific method   5
semiconductors   36
semimetals   14
silver   16, 29, 47
solids   29, 31, 34, 37, 39, 46, 54
solubility   37
solutions   40, 42, 44, 46, 47, 53
subatomic particles   12, 13, 21
sublimation   39
sugar   28, 37, 41, 46, 48, 58
sulfuric acid   42, 44
temperature   6, 10, 29, 31, 36, 37, 38,
   39, 40, 49, 55, 57
testing   6, 40
theory   7, 27
thermometer   10, 36
vapor   38, 39, 46, 56
variable   7
volume   29, 30, 33, 34
water   10, 18, 19, 21, 26, 28, 29, 30,
   31, 34, 35, 38, 39, 40, 41, 42, 43, 45,
   46, 47, 48, 52, 53, 54, 55, 58
weight   9, 10, 15, 19, 32, 33